INSTRUCTIONS

MAD LIBS® is a game for people who don't like games! It can be played by one, two, three, four, or forty.

• RIDICULOUSLY SIMPLE DIRECTIONS

In this tablet you will find stories containing blank spaces where words are left out. One player, the READER, selects one of these stories. The READER does not tell anyone what the story is about. Instead, he/she asks the other players, the WRITERS, to give him/her words. These words are used to fill in the blank spaces in the story.

• TO PLAY

The READER asks each WRITER in turn to call out a word—an adjective or a noun or whatever the space calls for—and uses them to fill in the blank spaces in the story. The result is a MAD LIBS® game.

When the READER then reads the completed MAD LIBS® game to the other players, they will discover that they have written a story that is fantastic, screamingly funny, shocking, silly, crazy, or just plain dumb—depending upon which words each WRITER called out.

• EXAMPLE (*Before* and *After*)

"______________ !" he said ______________
EXCLAMATION ADVERB

as he jumped into his convertible ______________ and
NOUN

drove off with his ______________ wife.
ADJECTIVE

"OUCH !" he said STUPIDLY
EXCLAMATION ADVERB

as he jumped into his convertible CAT and
NOUN

drove off with his BRAVE wife.
ADJECTIVE

MAD LIBS®

QUICK REVIEW

In case you have forgotten what adjectives, adverbs, nouns, and verbs are, here is a quick review:

An ADJECTIVE describes something or somebody. *Lumpy*, *soft*, *ugly*, *messy*, and *short* are adjectives.

An ADVERB tells how something is done. It modifies a verb and usually ends in "ly." *Modestly*, *stupidly*, *greedily*, and *carefully* are adverbs.

A NOUN is the name of a person, place, or thing. *Sidewalk*, *umbrella*, *bridle*, *bathtub*, and *nose* are nouns.

A VERB is an action word. *Run*, *pitch*, *jump*, and *swim* are verbs. Put the verbs in past tense if the directions say PAST TENSE. *Ran*, *pitched*, *jumped*, and *swam* are verbs in the past tense.

When we ask for A PLACE, we mean any sort of place: a country or city (*Spain*, *Cleveland*) or a room (*bathroom*, *kitchen*).

An EXCLAMATION or SILLY WORD is any sort of funny sound, gasp, grunt, or outcry, like *Wow!*, *Ouch!*, *Whomp!*, *Ick!*, and *Gadzooks!*

When we ask for specific words, like a NUMBER, a COLOR, an ANIMAL, or a PART OF THE BODY, we mean a word that is one of those things, like *seven*, *blue*, *horse*, or *head*.

When we ask for a PLURAL, it means more than one. For example, *cat* pluralized is *cats*.

MAD LIBS® is fun to play with friends, but you can also play it by yourself! To begin with, DO NOT look at the story on the page below. Fill in the blanks on this page with the words called for. Then, using the words you have selected, fill in the blank spaces in the story.

Now you've created your own hilarious MAD LIBS® game!

AIRPORT SECURITY CHECKLIST

ADJECTIVE ____________________

VERB ____________________

ADJECTIVE ____________________

ADJECTIVE ____________________

NOUN ____________________

VERB ____________________

TYPE OF LIQUID ____________________

NUMBER ____________________

NUMBER ____________________

VERB ____________________

ADVERB ____________________

PLURAL NOUN ____________________

PLURAL NOUN ____________________

PLURAL NOUN ____________________

ARTICLE OF CLOTHING ____________________

VERB ____________________

ADJECTIVE ____________________

PART OF THE BODY ____________________

MAD LIBS®

AIRPORT SECURITY CHECKLIST

So you've finally made it to the ___________ (ADJECTIVE) day—you're about to ___________ (VERB) to a faraway destination! The last thing you need is a/an ___________ (ADJECTIVE) situation when going through airport security. Here is a/an ___________ (ADJECTIVE) list to help you get through with no issues!

1. Be sure you have your ___________ (NOUN) and ticket ready to ___________ (VERB) to the agent.
2. Don't forget to throw out any bottles of ___________ (TYPE OF LIQUID) that exceed ___________ (NUMBER) ounces.
3. Don't get stuck waiting ___________ (NUMBER) hours in line! ___________ (VERB) through the line as ___________ (ADVERB) as possible.
4. Remove your ___________ (PLURAL NOUN) and put any ___________ (PLURAL NOUN) in the bins.
5. Make sure you don't have any metal ___________ (PLURAL NOUN) in your ___________ (ARTICLE OF CLOTHING), or else the agents will ___________ (VERB) you.

Follow these ___________ (ADJECTIVE) rules and you should get through airport security in the blink of a/an ___________ (PART OF THE BODY).

MAD LIBS® is fun to play with friends, but you can also play it by yourself! To begin with, DO NOT look at the story on the page below. Fill in the blanks on this page with the words called for. Then, using the words you have selected, fill in the blank spaces in the story.

Now you've created your own hilarious MAD LIBS® game!

THE BUS TRIP OF DOOM

NUMBER ____________

COLOR ____________

CITY ____________

ADJECTIVE ____________

VERB ____________

ADJECTIVE ____________

VERB (PAST TENSE) ____________

NOUN ____________

PART OF THE BODY (PLURAL) ____________

ADJECTIVE ____________

VERB (PAST TENSE) ____________

ADJECTIVE ____________

NOUN ____________

NOUN ____________

NUMBER ____________

VERB ____________

VERB ____________

MAD LIBS®

THE BUS TRIP OF DOOM

I arrived at the bus terminal at ______________ (NUMBER) a.m. to catch the ______________ (COLOR) Line Bus to ______________ (CITY). Little did I know I was in for a/an ______________ (ADJECTIVE) journey! Before we could even ______________ (VERB) the bus, we had to wait in a/an ______________ (ADJECTIVE) line. When it was time to board, everyone in line pushed and ______________ (VERB (PAST TENSE)) their way to the entrance. I settled into my ______________ (NOUN), put headphones in my ______________ (PART OF THE BODY (PLURAL)), and tried to relax. Unfortunately, the ______________ (ADJECTIVE) person next to me ______________ (VERB (PAST TENSE)) loudly the entire trip. Just when I thought the journey couldn't get any more ______________ (ADJECTIVE), the bus's ______________ (NOUN) started smoking. The whole bus smelled like a/an ______________ (NOUN)! After we exited the bus and waited on the side of the road for ______________ (NUMBER) hours, another bus came to ______________ (VERB) us. By the time we arrived, I promised myself I would never, ever ______________ (VERB) a bus again.

MAD LIBS® is fun to play with friends, but you can also play it by yourself! To begin with, DO NOT look at the story on the page below. Fill in the blanks on this page with the words called for. Then, using the words you have selected, fill in the blank spaces in the story.

Now you've created your own hilarious MAD LIBS® game!

TRAPPED IN THE BACK SEAT

VEHICLE ________________

PERSON IN ROOM ________________

PERSON IN ROOM ________________

ADJECTIVE ________________

VERB ________________

VERB ENDING IN "ING" ________________

VERB ________________

PART OF THE BODY (PLURAL) ________________

VERB ________________

TYPE OF FOOD ________________

NOUN ________________

ADJECTIVE ________________

NUMBER ________________

ADJECTIVE ________________

PART OF THE BODY (PLURAL) ________________

MAD LIBS®

TRAPPED IN THE BACK SEAT

Here I am, trapped in the back seat of the family ______________ (VEHICLE) again, stuck between ______________ (PERSON IN ROOM) and ______________ (PERSON IN ROOM). These two are such ______________ (ADJECTIVE) travel companions, they ______________ (VERB) me crazy! One has to be ______________ (VERB ENDING IN "ING") next to the window or else they ______________ (VERB) all over the back seat. The other has very smelly ______________ (PART OF THE BODY (PLURAL)). I try to ______________ (VERB) my nose, but it still smells like ______________ (TYPE OF FOOD). Maybe I'll see if we can put some ______________ (NOUN) on the radio. ______________ (ADJECTIVE) songs might distract me from this misery. I can't believe we still have ______________ (NUMBER) hours left! I will be so ______________ (ADJECTIVE) when this ride is finally over. I'm so cramped back here, I can't even feel my ______________ (PART OF THE BODY (PLURAL)).

MAD LIBS® is fun to play with friends, but you can also play it by yourself! To begin with, DO NOT look at the story on the page below. Fill in the blanks on this page with the words called for. Then, using the words you have selected, fill in the blank spaces in the story.

Now you've created your own hilarious MAD LIBS® game!

GOURMET AT 30,000 FEET

ADJECTIVE ______________________

PART OF THE BODY ______________________

NUMBER ______________________

NOUN ______________________

ADJECTIVE ______________________

NOUN ______________________

PLURAL NOUN ______________________

ADJECTIVE ______________________

TYPE OF FOOD ______________________

ADJECTIVE ______________________

ADJECTIVE ______________________

COLOR ______________________

NOUN ______________________

ADJECTIVE ______________________

TYPE OF LIQUID ______________________

ADJECTIVE ______________________

NUMBER ______________________

MAD LIBS®

GOURMET AT 30,000 FEET

By the time I settled into my ________________ (ADJECTIVE) seat, my ________________ (PART OF THE BODY) was growling. At ______________ (NUMBER) feet, the pilot finally turned off the "Fasten Your ______________ (NOUN)" sign, and meal service began. I was excited to dine on a/an ______________ (ADJECTIVE) meal in the clouds! I pulled down the ______________ (NOUN) from the seat in front of me as the flight attendants wheeled their ______________ (PLURAL NOUN) down the aisle. My choices were ______________ (ADJECTIVE) chicken, spicy ______________ (TYPE OF FOOD), or ______________ (ADJECTIVE) vegetables. I went with the chicken, and it was ________________ (ADJECTIVE)! It was covered in a/an ______________ (COLOR) sauce and smelled like ________________ (NOUN). My meal came with a side of ______________ (ADJECTIVE) bread and a hot cup of ______________ (TYPE OF LIQUID). I was hoping dessert would be more ________________ (ADJECTIVE), but it still tasted good. If this were a restaurant on the ground, I would give it __________ (NUMBER) stars!

MAD LIBS® is fun to play with friends, but you can also play it by yourself! To begin with, DO NOT look at the story on the page below. Fill in the blanks on this page with the words called for. Then, using the words you have selected, fill in the blank spaces in the story.

Now you've created your own hilarious MAD LIBS® game!

WHICH TRIP DO I PICK?

NUMBER ______________________

ADJECTIVE ______________________

ADJECTIVE ______________________

NOUN ______________________

CITY ______________________

NUMBER ______________________

NOUN ______________________

VERB ______________________

NOUN ______________________

PLURAL NOUN ______________________

PART OF THE BODY ______________________

ADJECTIVE ______________________

NOUN ______________________

ANIMAL ______________________

VERB ______________________

VERB ______________________

COUNTRY ______________________

MAD LIBS®

WHICH TRIP DO I PICK?

Congratulations! You're going on a fabulous ______________ -day
NUMBER

vacation! But which ______________ trip is right for you?
ADJECTIVE

- Do you like museums with ______________ art? Are you inspired by fountains and statues carved out of ______________? If so, you should travel to ______________!
  (ADJECTIVE) (NOUN) (CITY)

- Could you spend ______________ hours lying in the sand reading a/an ______________? Does the thought of seafood for every meal make your mouth ______________? If so, you should travel to ______________ Beach!
  (NUMBER) (NOUN) (VERB) (NOUN)

- Does flying down the slopes on a pair of ______________ make your ______________ race? Does the ______________ mountain air on your face refresh you? If so, you should travel to ______________ Mountain!
  (PLURAL NOUN) (PART OF THE BODY) (ADJECTIVE) (NOUN)

- Imagine seeing a real-life ______________ in the wild. Would you like to ______________ lions and elephants? Could you ______________ in a tent in the bush? If so, you should go on a safari to ______________!
  (ANIMAL) (VERB) (VERB) (COUNTRY)

MAD LIBS® is fun to play with friends, but you can also play it by yourself! To begin with, DO NOT look at the story on the page below. Fill in the blanks on this page with the words called for. Then, using the words you have selected, fill in the blank spaces in the story.

Now you've created your own hilarious MAD LIBS® game!

WHICH LINE IS WHICH?

ADJECTIVE ________________

OCCUPATION ________________

ADJECTIVE ________________

VERB ENDING IN "ING" ________________

NUMBER ________________

NOUN ________________

NUMBER ________________

ADJECTIVE ________________

NOUN ________________

COLOR ________________

NUMBER ________________

NUMBER ________________

VERB ________________

OCCUPATION ________________

VERB ENDING IN "ING" ________________

PLURAL NOUN ________________

ADJECTIVE ________________

MAD LIBS®

WHICH LINE IS WHICH?

________ afternoon, passengers. This is your ________
ADJECTIVE OCCUPATION

speaking. Our train is stopped because of a/an ________
ADJECTIVE

passenger at the next station. We should be ________
VERB ENDING IN "ING"

in about ________ minutes. We thank you for your
NUMBER

________. Additionally, this train will be skipping the next
NOUN

________ stops due to ________ construction. We
NUMBER ADJECTIVE

apologize for the ________. Also, the ________ train is
NOUN COLOR

running on the ________ train line this week, and service will
NUMBER

stop at ________ p.m. every night. Lastly, if you see
NUMBER

something suspicious, ________ something to a police
VERB

officer or ________. Thank you for ________ the
OCCUPATION VERB ENDING IN "ING"

subway, and please remember to bring all ________ with you
PLURAL NOUN

when exiting the train. Have a/an ________ day.
ADJECTIVE

MAD LIBS® is fun to play with friends, but you can also play it by yourself! To begin with, DO NOT look at the story on the page below. Fill in the blanks on this page with the words called for. Then, using the words you have selected, fill in the blank spaces in the story.

Now you've created your own hilarious MAD LIBS® game!

FLYING LIKE ROYALTY

ADJECTIVE ______________________

NUMBER ______________________

VEHICLE ______________________

NOUN ______________________

ADJECTIVE ______________________

VERB ______________________

ADJECTIVE ______________________

TYPE OF FOOD (PLURAL) ______________________

ADJECTIVE ______________________

EXCLAMATION ______________________

PART OF THE BODY (PLURAL) ______________________

TYPE OF LIQUID ______________________

NUMBER ______________________

ADJECTIVE ______________________

NUMBER ______________________

ADVERB ______________________

MAD LIBS®

FLYING LIKE ROYALTY

My ____________ experience flying first class began ____________
ADJECTIVE NUMBER
hours before I even got on the plane. A/An ____________ picked me
VEHICLE
up at my ____________ and brought me to the airport. Next, I
NOUN
had a/an ____________ assistant ____________ me through
ADJECTIVE VERB
the security line and straight to a members-only lounge. The lounge
had ____________ food and beverage service, including plates of
ADJECTIVE
yummy ____________. Once on the plane, I was shown to
TYPE OF FOOD (PLURAL)
my extremely ____________ seat. ____________! This seat was so
ADJECTIVE EXCLAMATION
spacious, I could stretch my ____________ all the way out.
PART OF THE BODY (PLURAL)
I was served a glass of sparkling ____________ before
TYPE OF LIQUID
we took off. Once we were in the air, I was immediately served a/an
____________-course meal. Later, I drifted off to sleep and thought
NUMBER
about the ____________ passengers stuck in economy. If I had
ADJECTIVE
____________ dollars, I'd ____________ fly first class every time!
NUMBER ADVERB

MAD LIBS® is fun to play with friends, but you can also play it by yourself! To begin with, DO NOT look at the story on the page below. Fill in the blanks on this page with the words called for. Then, using the words you have selected, fill in the blank spaces in the story.

Now you've created your own hilarious MAD LIBS® game!

RUSHING THROUGH RUSH HOUR

VERB ENDING IN "ING" ____________________

NOUN ____________________

EXCLAMATION ____________________

ADJECTIVE ____________________

ADJECTIVE ____________________

PLURAL NOUN ____________________

ADJECTIVE ____________________

NUMBER ____________________

VEHICLE ____________________

NOUN ____________________

ADJECTIVE ____________________

PART OF THE BODY ____________________

CELEBRITY ____________________

NOUN ____________________

ADJECTIVE ____________________

ADJECTIVE ____________________

MAD LIBS®

RUSHING THROUGH RUSH HOUR

The sun was ________________ (VERB ENDING IN "ING") down, and we had to get home before dark. We turned on the ________________ (NOUN) and listened to the traffic report. ________________ (EXCLAMATION)! There was traffic on every ________________ (ADJECTIVE) highway. We tried taking a/an ________________ (ADJECTIVE) -cut through downtown, but there were long lines of ________________ (PLURAL NOUN) on every road. It took us one ________________ (ADJECTIVE) hour to drive ________________ (NUMBER) miles, and the ________________ (VEHICLE) behind us honked its ________________ (NOUN) the whole time. The noise was so ________________ (ADJECTIVE), I thought I was going to lose my ________________ (PART OF THE BODY)! We turned on the radio and listened to music by ________________ (CELEBRITY) to drown out the noise. But traffic was still a waking ________________ (NOUN)! Finally, we got on a/an ________________ (ADJECTIVE) country road that was less crowded. After a long and ________________ (ADJECTIVE) drive, it sure was nice to be home!

MAD LIBS® is fun to play with friends, but you can also play it by yourself! To begin with, DO NOT look at the story on the page below. Fill in the blanks on this page with the words called for. Then, using the words you have selected, fill in the blank spaces in the story.

Now you've created your own hilarious MAD LIBS® game!

TALES FROM THE BUS STOP

TYPE OF FOOD ____________________

TYPE OF LIQUID ____________________

ADVERB ____________________

PLURAL NOUN ____________________

NUMBER ____________________

ADJECTIVE ____________________

VERB (PAST TENSE) ____________________

PLURAL NOUN ____________________

ADJECTIVE ____________________

NOUN ____________________

ADJECTIVE ____________________

NOUN ____________________

PART OF THE BODY ____________________

ADVERB ____________________

VEHICLE ____________________

MAD LIBS®

TALES FROM THE BUS STOP

I ate my morning meal of ______________ (TYPE OF FOOD), gulped down a glass of ______________ (TYPE OF LIQUID), and rushed out the door to catch the bus. I ran to the bus stop as ______________ (ADVERB) as possible only to see a crowd of ______________ (PLURAL NOUN) gathered on the curb. The bus was running ______________ (NUMBER) minutes late. I started to feel ______________ (ADJECTIVE) when all of a sudden the bus arrived! We all ______________ (VERB (PAST TENSE)) onto the bus and tried to get ______________ (PLURAL NOUN) as close to the back as possible. I got stuck between a/an ______________ (ADJECTIVE) person and someone who talked loudly on her ______________ (NOUN) the entire ride. That was ______________ (ADJECTIVE) enough, and then I noticed I was sitting on a piece of chewed-up ______________ (NOUN). My ______________ (PART OF THE BODY) was stuck to the seat! When we ______________ (ADVERB) got to our destination, I thought, *I need to get my own* ______________ (VEHICLE)*!*

MAD LIBS® is fun to play with friends, but you can also play it by yourself! To begin with, DO NOT look at the story on the page below. Fill in the blanks on this page with the words called for. Then, using the words you have selected, fill in the blank spaces in the story.

Now you've created your own hilarious MAD LIBS® game!

RED-EYE NIGHTMARE

NUMBER ____________________

COUNTRY ____________________

PART OF THE BODY (PLURAL) ____________________

ADJECTIVE ____________________

NOUN ____________________

PART OF THE BODY (PLURAL) ____________________

PLURAL NOUN ____________________

ADVERB ____________________

EXCLAMATION ____________________

ADJECTIVE ____________________

PLURAL NOUN ____________________

VERB ____________________

NOUN ____________________

PART OF THE BODY ____________________

VERB ENDING IN "ING" ____________________

TYPE OF LIQUID ____________________

VERB ____________________

ADJECTIVE ____________________

MAD LIBS®

RED-EYE NIGHTMARE

It was close to midnight when I finally boarded flight number ______________ (NUMBER) to ______________ (COUNTRY). I was excited to close my ______________ (PART OF THE BODY (PLURAL)) and drift off to sleep for the ______________ (ADJECTIVE) flight. When I got to my seat, there was a/an ______________ (NOUN) for my eyes, ______________ (PART OF THE BODY (PLURAL))-plugs, and a blanket made of ______________ (PLURAL NOUN). That's when I realized that my seat did not ______________ (ADVERB) recline. ______________ (EXCLAMATION)! This was going to be a rough and ______________ (ADJECTIVE) flight. Thankfully the flight attendants turned the ______________ (PLURAL NOUN) off in the cabin, and it was dark enough to ______________ (VERB). But every time the ______________ (NOUN) cart went by, it hit me in the ______________ (PART OF THE BODY) and woke me up. Then, the person next to me started ______________ (VERB ENDING IN "ING") up phlegm and ______________ (TYPE OF LIQUID)! Gross! I managed to ______________ (VERB) a little on the flight, but I must have looked ______________ (ADJECTIVE) by the time I arrived.

MAD LIBS® is fun to play with friends, but you can also play it by yourself! To begin with, DO NOT look at the story on the page below. Fill in the blanks on this page with the words called for. Then, using the words you have selected, fill in the blank spaces in the story.

Now you've created your own hilarious MAD LIBS® game!

A GLOBAL MENU

ADJECTIVE ______________________

VERB ______________________

ADJECTIVE ______________________

NOUN ______________________

NOUN ______________________

ADJECTIVE ______________________

PLURAL NOUN ______________________

COLOR ______________________

NUMBER ______________________

TYPE OF LIQUID ______________________

ADJECTIVE ______________________

VERB ______________________

VERB ______________________

PLURAL NOUN ______________________

TYPE OF FOOD ______________________

ADJECTIVE ______________________

VERB ______________________

PLURAL NOUN ______________________

MAD LIBS®

A GLOBAL MENU

Welcome to our ______________ restaurant, where we are proud to
ADJECTIVE

______________ our country's famous cuisine. Read the menu to
VERB

discover ______________ local treats.
ADJECTIVE

- **Fried** ______________**:** This dish is famous for its ______________
NOUN / NOUN
sauce and ______________ flavor. Served with plenty of
ADJECTIVE
______________ on the side!
PLURAL NOUN
- **Steamed** ______________ **Fish:** We cook our fish for ______________
COLOR / NUMBER
minutes over an open flame, then marinate it in ______________
TYPE OF LIQUID
for a tangy finish.
- **Grilled** ______________ **Chicken:** First, we ______________ the
ADJECTIVE / VERB
chicken so it is moist. Then, we ______________ it at a high
VERB
temperature and serve it on a bed of ______________.
PLURAL NOUN
- ______________ **Soup:** One of the most ______________ soups
TYPE OF FOOD / ADJECTIVE
in our country! This broth is so spicy, people often ______________
VERB
their tongues.

We hope you enjoy the delicious ______________ that our country
PLURAL NOUN

has to offer!

MAD LIBS® is fun to play with friends, but you can also play it by yourself! To begin with, DO NOT look at the story on the page below. Fill in the blanks on this page with the words called for. Then, using the words you have selected, fill in the blank spaces in the story.

Now you've created your own hilarious MAD LIBS® game!

THE ESSENTIAL PACKING LIST

ADJECTIVE ________________

VERB ________________

NOUN ________________

PART OF THE BODY ________________

ADJECTIVE ________________

VERB ENDING IN "ING" ________________

PLURAL NOUN ________________

PLURAL NOUN ________________

OCCUPATION ________________

ANIMAL ________________

PART OF THE BODY ________________

TYPE OF FOOD ________________

TYPE OF LIQUID ________________

NOUN ________________

CELEBRITY ________________

ADJECTIVE ________________

PART OF THE BODY ________________

PLURAL NOUN ________________

MAD LIBS®

THE ESSENTIAL PACKING LIST

Whether you're a/an ____________ (ADJECTIVE) traveler or a first-time adventurer, this packing checklist will help you ____________ (VERB) for your next journey:

1. Tooth- ____________ (NOUN) and ____________ (PART OF THE BODY) -wash. Nobody likes ____________ (ADJECTIVE) breath in the morning.
2. A guide book for sight- ____________ (VERB ENDING IN "ING"). You want to be sure to visit the best local ____________ (PLURAL NOUN) during your trip.
3. Loose ____________ (PLURAL NOUN) for tipping the ____________ (OCCUPATION) at your hotel
4. Sunscreen and ____________ (ANIMAL) spray to protect your ____________ (PART OF THE BODY) from the elements
5. ____________ (TYPE OF FOOD) -Mix, plenty of bottled ____________ (TYPE OF LIQUID), and ____________ (NOUN) bars for when you get the travel munchies
6. Music by ____________ (CELEBRITY) and a good set of headphones
7. A/An ____________ (ADJECTIVE) pair of walking shoes
8. An open ____________ (PART OF THE BODY)! For the best traveling experience, meet new ____________ (PLURAL NOUN) and try new experiences.

MAD LIBS® is fun to play with friends, but you can also play it by yourself! To begin with, DO NOT look at the story on the page below. Fill in the blanks on this page with the words called for. Then, using the words you have selected, fill in the blank spaces in the story.

Now you've created your own hilarious MAD LIBS® game!

TO GRANDMOTHER'S HOUSE WE GO

NOUN ____________

A PLACE ____________

ANIMAL ____________

VERB ____________

COLOR ____________

NOUN ____________

NOUN ____________

PART OF THE BODY (PLURAL) ____________

NOUN ____________

PERSON IN ROOM ____________

EXCLAMATION ____________

PLURAL NOUN ____________

TYPE OF FOOD ____________

NOUN ____________

ARTICLE OF CLOTHING ____________

EXCLAMATION ____________

TYPE OF FOOD ____________

MAD LIBS
TO GRANDMOTHER'S HOUSE WE GO

Over the ______________, and through the wood,
NOUN

to Grandmother's ______________ we go.
A PLACE

The ______________ knows the way to ______________ the sleigh
ANIMAL VERB

through the ______________ and drifted snow.
COLOR

Over the river, and through the ______________—
NOUN

oh, how the ______________ does blow!
NOUN

It stings the ______________ and bites the nose
PART OF THE BODY (PLURAL)

as over the ______________ we go.
NOUN

Over the river, and through the wood—

when ______________ sees us come,
PERSON IN ROOM

she will say, "______________, dear, the ______________ are here,
EXCLAMATION PLURAL NOUN

bring a/an ______________ for everyone."
TYPE OF FOOD

Over the ______________, and through the wood—
NOUN

now Grandmother's ______________ I spy!
ARTICLE OF CLOTHING

______________ for the fun! Is the pudding done?
EXCLAMATION

Hurrah for the ______________ pie!
TYPE OF FOOD

MAD LIBS® is fun to play with friends, but you can also play it by yourself! To begin with, DO NOT look at the story on the page below. Fill in the blanks on this page with the words called for. Then, using the words you have selected, fill in the blank spaces in the story.

Now you've created your own hilarious MAD LIBS® game!

TIME ZONE TIZZY

VEHICLE ________________

COUNTRY ________________

VERB ________________

ADJECTIVE ________________

ADJECTIVE ________________

VERB ________________

TYPE OF FOOD ________________

TYPE OF LIQUID ________________

VERB (PAST TENSE) ________________

PART OF THE BODY (PLURAL) ________________

PERSON IN ROOM ________________

NOUN ________________

NOUN ________________

ARTICLE OF CLOTHING ________________

NUMBER ________________

ADJECTIVE ________________

MAD LIBS®

TIME ZONE TIZZY

It was Wednesday when my ____________ (VEHICLE) left for ____________ (COUNTRY). We didn't ____________ (VERB) until Friday morning. Talk about a/an ____________ (ADJECTIVE) flight! The sun was ____________ (ADJECTIVE) when I arrived, but I just wanted to go to bed and ____________ (VERB). I decided to get some ____________ (TYPE OF FOOD) and a hot cup of ____________ (TYPE OF LIQUID) to keep me awake, but that didn't work. By the time I ____________ (VERB (PAST TENSE)) to my hotel, I could barely keep my ____________ (PART OF THE BODY (PLURAL)) open. I wanted to call ____________ (PERSON IN ROOM) to say I'd made it safely, but I knew it was the middle of the ____________ (NOUN) back home. Finally, I was able to enjoy a hot ____________ (NOUN) in my room and change into a cozy ____________ (ARTICLE OF CLOTHING). It took me ____________ (NUMBER) days to get over my jet lag, but when I did, I had the most ____________ (ADJECTIVE) trip of my life!

MAD LIBS® is fun to play with friends, but you can also play it by yourself! To begin with, DO NOT look at the story on the page below. Fill in the blanks on this page with the words called for. Then, using the words you have selected, fill in the blank spaces in the story.

Now you've created your own hilarious MAD LIBS® game!

POSTCARD FROM PARADISE

PERSON IN ROOM ____________________

ADJECTIVE ____________________

COUNTRY ____________________

VERB ____________________

VEHICLE ____________________

TYPE OF FOOD ____________________

TYPE OF LIQUID ____________________

PERSON IN ROOM ____________________

ADJECTIVE ____________________

PLURAL NOUN ____________________

ADJECTIVE ____________________

ADJECTIVE ____________________

CELEBRITY ____________________

PLURAL NOUN ____________________

NOUN ____________________

VERB ____________________

NOUN ____________________

ANIMAL ____________________

PERSON IN ROOM ____________________

MAD LIBS®

POSTCARD FROM PARADISE

Dear ________________,
PERSON IN ROOM

I'm having the most ________________ time in ________________. I
ADJECTIVE / COUNTRY

miss you so much, I could ________________! The first day I was here,
VERB

I rode a/an ________________ to a local farm that grows ________________.
VEHICLE / TYPE OF FOOD

I drank the freshest ________________ in my life! ________________ is
TYPE OF LIQUID / PERSON IN ROOM

a/an ________________ travel buddy. We haven't had any fights or
ADJECTIVE

________________ at all! Our hotel is very ________________. The staff
PLURAL NOUN / ADJECTIVE

is so friendly and ________________, I feel like ________________!
ADJECTIVE / CELEBRITY

Before we leave, I want to see all the best ________________ near our
PLURAL NOUN

hotel. I am having so much ________________ that I don't want to
NOUN

________________ home! Please don't forget to water my ________________
VERB / NOUN

and feed my ________________. See you soon!
ANIMAL

Love,

____
PERSON IN ROOM

MAD LIBS® is fun to play with friends, but you can also play it by yourself! To begin with, DO NOT look at the story on the page below. Fill in the blanks on this page with the words called for. Then, using the words you have selected, fill in the blank spaces in the story.

Now you've created your own hilarious MAD LIBS® game!

LIFE AT SEA

ADJECTIVE ______________________

COUNTRY ______________________

ADJECTIVE ______________________

VERB (PAST TENSE) ______________________

NOUN ______________________

ARTICLE OF CLOTHING ______________________

VERB ______________________

TYPE OF FOOD (PLURAL) ______________________

ADJECTIVE ______________________

NOUN ______________________

PLURAL NOUN ______________________

COLOR ______________________

TYPE OF FOOD ______________________

OCCUPATION ______________________

CELEBRITY ______________________

ADVERB ______________________

ADJECTIVE ______________________

MAD LIBS®

LIFE AT SEA

Ahoy! I have just returned from a/an ______________ (ADJECTIVE) cruise around the coast of ______________ (COUNTRY). What a/an ______________ (ADJECTIVE) adventure! When we first ______________ (VERB (PAST TENSE)) the ship, we had to complete a safety ______________ (NOUN) and practice putting on a life ______________ (ARTICLE OF CLOTHING). I was worried that the waves would make me ______________ (VERB), but I felt perfectly fine. Afterward, I ordered a plate of ______________ (TYPE OF FOOD (PLURAL)) and brought it to my room. My cabin was nice and ______________ (ADJECTIVE)! It had a nice view of the ______________ (NOUN) and plenty of space for my ______________ (PLURAL NOUN). Every night, I wore ______________ (COLOR)-tie attire and dined on the finest ______________ (TYPE OF FOOD) I had ever eaten. I even got to meet the ______________ (OCCUPATION) who organized events, and a/an ______________ (CELEBRITY) impersonator who did live shows each night. I would ______________ (ADVERB) recommend this ______________ (ADJECTIVE) vacation to anyone.

MAD LIBS® is fun to play with friends, but you can also play it by yourself! To begin with, DO NOT look at the story on the page below. Fill in the blanks on this page with the words called for. Then, using the words you have selected, fill in the blank spaces in the story.

Now you've created your own hilarious MAD LIBS® game!

TWO WHEELS ARE BETTER THAN FOUR

ADJECTIVE ______________________

ADJECTIVE ______________________

VERB ENDING IN "ING" ______________________

NUMBER ______________________

ARTICLE OF CLOTHING ______________________

VERB ______________________

PART OF THE BODY ______________________

ADJECTIVE ______________________

PLURAL NOUN ______________________

VERB ______________________

PART OF THE BODY ______________________

VERB ______________________

ARTICLE OF CLOTHING ______________________

ADJECTIVE ______________________

ADJECTIVE ______________________

NOUN ______________________

MAD LIBS®

TWO WHEELS ARE BETTER THAN FOUR

Riding your bike is a fun and ______________ (ADJECTIVE) activity, but it can be very ______________ (ADJECTIVE). I've been ______________ (VERB ENDING IN "ING") my bike for ______________ (NUMBER) years and can give some great advice. First, always wear a/an ______________ (ARTICLE OF CLOTHING). You don't want to ______________ (VERB) an accident and injure your ______________ (PART OF THE BODY). Cycling when the weather is ______________ (ADJECTIVE) can also be tricky. Make sure you have at least two reflective ______________ (PLURAL NOUN) at all times. This will help cars ______________ (VERB) your bike in the rain. Always use ______________ (PART OF THE BODY) signals to indicate whether you want to ______________ (VERB) left or right. Wear a breathable ______________ (ARTICLE OF CLOTHING) so you don't get too ______________ (ADJECTIVE) on your ride. Lastly, make sure you have a/an ______________ (ADJECTIVE) lock for your bike. You don't want your favorite ______________ (NOUN) to get stolen!

MAD LIBS® is fun to play with friends, but you can also play it by yourself! To begin with, DO NOT look at the story on the page below. Fill in the blanks on this page with the words called for. Then, using the words you have selected, fill in the blank spaces in the story.

Now you've created your own hilarious MAD LIBS® game!

A WEATHER REPORT

PLURAL NOUN ____________

CITY ____________

NUMBER ____________

ADJECTIVE ____________

VERB (PAST TENSE) ____________

ADJECTIVE ____________

NOUN ____________

PLURAL NOUN ____________

NUMBER ____________

TYPE OF FOOD ____________

TYPE OF LIQUID ____________

VERB ____________

ADJECTIVE ____________

ADJECTIVE ____________

EXCLAMATION ____________

ADJECTIVE ____________

VERB ____________

PERSON IN ROOM ____________

MAD LIBS®

A WEATHER REPORT

Hello, ________________,
PLURAL NOUN

I am reporting to you live from the airport in ________________.
CITY

Since yesterday, we have received ________________ feet of snow with
NUMBER

________________ winds. All flights have been ________________,
ADJECTIVE VERB (PAST TENSE)

leaving passengers feeling ________________. A spokesperson from
ADJECTIVE

________________ Air promised that passengers will be issued ________________
NOUN PLURAL NOUN

for meals and hotels. I interviewed a passenger earlier who said she

hadn't slept for ________________ hours. Furthermore, the airport is running
NUMBER

dangerously low on ________________ and ________________.
TYPE OF FOOD TYPE OF LIQUID

Travelers hoping to ________________ to other destinations have had to
VERB

make ________________ plans. Many of the passengers I spoke with were
ADJECTIVE

tired and ________________. One man cried, "________________!" when
ADJECTIVE EXCLAMATION

I asked how he was feeling. The situation looks pretty ________________,
ADJECTIVE

and I will continue to ________________ any updates with our viewers.
VERB

Now back to you, ________________, in the studio!
PERSON IN ROOM

MAD LIBS® is fun to play with friends, but you can also play it by yourself! To begin with, DO NOT look at the story on the page below. Fill in the blanks on this page with the words called for. Then, using the words you have selected, fill in the blank spaces in the story.

Now you've created your own hilarious MAD LIBS® game!

CULTURE SHOCK!

ADJECTIVE ______________________

VERB ENDING IN "ING" ______________________

ADJECTIVE ______________________

ANIMAL (PLURAL) ______________________

VERB ______________________

PLURAL NOUN ______________________

VERB ______________________

PART OF THE BODY ______________________

TYPE OF FOOD ______________________

ADJECTIVE ______________________

VERB ______________________

NUMBER ______________________

ADJECTIVE ______________________

ADJECTIVE ______________________

MAD LIBS

CULTURE SHOCK!

I've already spent two ________________ weeks abroad and I'm still
ADJECTIVE

in shock! I was not ________________ the customs and traditions
VERB ENDING IN "ING"

overseas to be so different from our own. One thing I've found very

____________ is the local people's deep respect for ______________.
ADJECTIVE ANIMAL (PLURAL)

We deep-fry and ____________ those critters back home! Many of
VERB

the friends I've made have statues of ______________ in their homes.
PLURAL NOUN

And when you greet someone, you're supposed to ____________
VERB

with your ______________. How wonderful! I've also never eaten so
PART OF THE BODY

much ____________ in my life! It's the national dish, and it tastes
TYPE OF FOOD

very ____________. Every day, after lunch, people ____________
ADJECTIVE VERB

for at least ____________ hours. We should do that, too! I just love
NUMBER

how ______________ the locals have been. I am learning something
ADJECTIVE

____________ every day!
ADJECTIVE

MAD LIBS® is fun to play with friends, but you can also play it by yourself! To begin with, DO NOT look at the story on the page below. Fill in the blanks on this page with the words called for. Then, using the words you have selected, fill in the blank spaces in the story.

Now you've created your own hilarious MAD LIBS® game!

SAY WHAT?

COUNTRY ____________

PLURAL NOUN ____________

VERB ENDING IN "ING" ____________

VEHICLE ____________

ADJECTIVE ____________

NOUN ____________

NOUN ____________

TYPE OF BUILDING ____________

TYPE OF FOOD ____________

TYPE OF LIQUID ____________

PLURAL NOUN ____________

ADJECTIVE ____________

NOUN ____________

VERB ____________

EXCLAMATION ____________

VERB ____________

MAD LIBS®

SAY WHAT?

When I landed in ________________ (COUNTRY), I realized I had forgotten all my ________________ (PLURAL NOUN) at home! Instead of ________________ (VERB ENDING IN "ING") straight to my hotel, I asked the ________________ (VEHICLE) driver to take me shopping. She looked at me like I was ________________ (ADJECTIVE)! I thought maybe she couldn't understand me, so I pulled out a/an ________________ (NOUN) to show her where I needed to go. Instead of driving to the ________________ (NOUN), she drove me to a/an ________________ (TYPE OF BUILDING) in the middle of nowhere! They sold ________________ (TYPE OF FOOD), ________________ (TYPE OF LIQUID), ________________ (PLURAL NOUN), and not much else. I decided to ask a/an ________________ (ADJECTIVE)-looking woman for directions to the nearest ________________ (NOUN). I tried to ________________ (VERB) the translation app on my phone, but the woman just looked at me and said, "________________ (EXCLAMATION)!" I guess I should really ________________ (VERB) the language before I travel!

MAD LIBS® is fun to play with friends, but you can also play it by yourself! To begin with, DO NOT look at the story on the page below. Fill in the blanks on this page with the words called for. Then, using the words you have selected, fill in the blank spaces in the story.

Now you've created your own hilarious MAD LIBS® game!

YOU'VE ARRIVED!

NUMBER ________________

ADJECTIVE ________________

VERB ________________

VEHICLE ________________

PLURAL NOUN ________________

NOUN ________________

VERB ________________

OCCUPATION ________________

VERB ________________

VERB ________________

PLURAL NOUN ________________

ADJECTIVE ________________

ADJECTIVE ________________

PERSON IN ROOM ________________

VERB ________________

ADJECTIVE ________________

ADJECTIVE ________________

MAD LIBS®

YOU'VE ARRIVED!

After ______________ hours of traveling, you've finally arrived at your
NUMBER

______________ destination. What are you supposed to ______________ now?
ADJECTIVE VERB

1. Catch a/an ______________ to your hotel. Don't forget to carry
VEHICLE

______________ to tip the driver!
PLURAL NOUN

2. Check into your hotel at the front ______________. Always
NOUN

______________ for an upgrade!
VERB

3. Ask the ______________ at your hotel for some restaurant
OCCUPATION

recommendations. They can ______________ a reservation for you.
VERB

4. ______________ your phone until it's 100 percent charged. Make
VERB

sure you have plenty of room for ______________ on your camera.
PLURAL NOUN

5. Have ______________ conversations with locals. Learn
ADJECTIVE

______________ phrases to help you.
ADJECTIVE

6. Call ______________ to let them know you made it safely.
PERSON IN ROOM

______________ photos to your friends and family so they can see
VERB

your ______________ adventures!
ADJECTIVE

Stay safe, and have a/an ______________ time!
ADJECTIVE

Join the millions of Mad Libs fans creating wacky and wonderful stories on our apps!

Download Mad Libs today!